D1325220

1935 if you wanted to
read a good book, you needed
either a lot of money or a library card.
Cheap paperbacks were available, but their
poor production generally mirrored the quality
between the covers. One weekend that year,
Allen Lane, Managing Director of The Bodley Head,
having spent the weekend visiting Agatha Christie,
found himself on a platform at Exeter station trying to
find something to read for his journey back to London.
He was appalled by the quality of the material he had to
choose from. Everything that Allen Lane achieved from that
day until his death in 1970 was based on a passionate belief
in the existence of 'a vast reading public for *intelligent*
books at a low price'. The result of his momentous vision
was the birth not only of Penguin, but of the 'paperback
revolution'. Quality writing became available for the price of
a packet of cigarettes, literature became a mass medium
for the first time, a nation of book-borrowers became a
nation of book-buyers – and the very concept of book
publishing was changed for ever. Those founding
principles – of quality and value, with an overarching
belief in the fundamental importance of reading –
have guided everything the company has
done since 1935. Sir Allen Lane's
pioneering spirit is still very much alive
at Penguin in 2005. Here's to
the next 70 years!

MORE THAN A BUSINESS

'We decided it was time to end the almost customary half-hearted manner in which cheap editions were produced – as though the only people who could possibly want cheap editions must belong to a lower order of intelligence. We, however, believed in the existence in this country of a vast reading public for intelligent books at a low price, and staked everything on it'
Sir Allen Lane, 1902–1970

'The Penguin Books are splendid value for sixpence, so splendid that if other publishers had any sense they would combine against them and suppress them'
George Orwell

'More than a business … a national cultural asset'
Guardian

'When you look at the whole Penguin achievement you know that it constitutes, in action, one of the more democratic successes of our recent social history'
Richard Hoggart

Artists and Models

ANAÏS NIN

PENGUIN BOOKS

PENGUIN BOOKS

Published by the Penguin Group
Penguin Books Ltd, 80 Strand, London WC2R ORL, England
Penguin Group (USA) Inc., 375 Hudson Street, New York, New York 10014, USA
Penguin Group (Canada), 10 Alcorn Avenue, Toronto, Ontario, Canada M4V 3B2
(a division of Pearson Penguin Canada Inc.)
Penguin Ireland, 25 St Stephen's Green, Dublin 2, Ireland
(a division of Penguin Books Ltd)
Penguin Group (Australia), 250 Camberwell Road, Camberwell, Victoria 3124,
Australia (a division of Pearson Australia Group Pty Ltd)
Penguin Books India Pvt Ltd, 11 Community Centre,
Panchsheel Park, New Delhi – 110 017, India
Penguin Group (NZ), cnr Airborne and Rosedale Roads, Albany,
Auckland 1310, New Zealand (a division of Pearson New Zealand Ltd)
Penguin Books (South Africa) (Pty) Ltd, 24 Sturdee Avenue,
Rosebank 2196, South Africa

Penguin Books Ltd, Registered Offices: 80 Strand, London WC2R ORL, England

www.penguin.com

The Delta of Venus first published in Great Britain 1978
First published in Penguin Books 1990
Little Birds first published in Great Britain 1979
First published in Penguin Books 1990
This selection published as a Pocket Penguin 2005

1

Set in 10.5/12.5pt Monotype Dante
Typeset by Palimpsest Book Production Limited
Polmont, Stirlingshire
Printed in England by Clays Ltd, St Ives plc

Contents

Artists and Models

One morning I was called to a studio in Greenwich Village, where a sculptor was beginning a statuette. His name was Millard. He already had a rough version of the figure he wanted and had reached the stage where he needed a model.

The statuette was wearing a clinging dress, and the body showed through in every line and curve. The sculptor asked me to undress completely because he could not work otherwise. He seemed so absorbed by the statuette and looked at me so absently that I was able to undress and take the pose without hesitation. Although I was quite innocent at that time, he made me feel as if my body were no different than my face, as if I were the same as the statuette.

As Millard worked, he talked about his former life in Montparnasse, and the time passed quickly. I didn't know if his stories were meant to affect my imagination, but he showed no signs of being interested in me. He enjoyed recreating the atmosphere of Montparnasse for his own sake. This is one of the stories he told me:

'The wife of one of the modern painters was a nymphomaniac. She was tubercular, I believe. She had a chalk-white face, burning black eyes deeply sunk in her face, with eyelids painted green. She had a voluptuous figure, which she covered very sleekly in black satin. Her waist was small in proportion to the rest of her body. Around her waist she wore a huge Greek silver belt, about six inches wide, studded with stones. The belt was fascinating. It was like the belt of a slave. One felt that deep down she *was* a slave – to her sexual hunger. One felt that all one had to do was to grip the belt and open it for her to fall into one's arms. It was very much like the chastity belt they showed in the Musée Cluny, which the crusaders were said to have put on their wives, a very wide silver belt with a hanging appendage that covered the sex and locked it up for the duration of their crusades. Someone told me the delightful story of a crusader who had put a chastity belt on his wife and left the key in care of his best friend in case of his death. He had barely ridden away a few miles when he saw his friend riding furiously after him, calling out, "You gave me the wrong key!"

'Such were the feelings that the belt of Louise inspired in everyone. Seeing her arrive at a café, her hungry eyes looking us over, searching for a response, an invitation to sit down, we knew she was out on a hunt for the day. Her husband could not help knowing about this. He was a pitiful figure, always looking for her, being told by his friends that she was at another café and then another, where he would go, which gave her time to steal off to a hotel room with someone. Then everyone would try to let her know where her husband was looking for her. Finally, in desperation, he began to beg his best friends to take her, so that at least she would not fall into strangers' hands.

'He had a fear of strangers, of South Americans in particular, and of Negroes and Cubans. He had heard remarks about their extraordinary sexual powers and felt that, if his wife fell into their hands, she would never return to him. Louise, however, after having slept with all his best friends, finally did meet one of the strangers.

'He was a Cuban, a tremendous brown man, extraordinarily handsome, with long, straight hair like a Hindu's and beautifully full, noble features. He would practically live at the Dome until he found a woman he wanted. And then they would disappear for two or three days, locked up in a hotel room, and not reappear until they were both satiated. He believed in making such a thorough feast of a woman that neither one wanted to see the other again. Only when this was over would he be seen sitting in the café again, conversing brilliantly. He was, in addition, a remarkable fresco painter.

'When he and Louise met, they immediately went off together. Antonio was powerfully fascinated by the whiteness of her skin, the abundance of her breasts, her slender waist, her long, straight, heavy blond hair. And she was fascinated by his head and powerful body, by his slowness and ease. Everything made him laugh. He gave one the feeling that the whole world was now shut out and only this sensual feast existed, that there would be no tomorrows, no meetings with anyone else – that there was only this room, this afternoon, this bed.

'When she stood by the big iron bed, waiting, he said, "Keep your belt on." And he began by slowly tearing her dress from around it. Calmly and with no effort, he tore it into shreds as if it were made of paper. Louise was trembling at the strength of his hands. She stood naked now except for the heavy silver belt. He loosened her hair over her shoulders. And only then did he bend her back on the bed and kiss her interminably, his hands over her breasts. She felt the painful weight both of the silver belt and of his hands pressing so hard on her naked flesh. Her sexual hunger was rising like madness to her head, blinding her. It was so urgent that she could not wait. She could not

3

even wait until he undressed. But Antonio ignored her movements of impatience. He not only continued to kiss her as if he were drinking her whole mouth, tongue, breath, into his big dark mouth, but his hands mauled her, pressed deeply into her flesh, leaving marks and pain everywhere. She was moist and trembling, opening her legs and trying to climb over him. She tried to open his pants.

'"There is time," he said. "There is plenty of time. We are going to stay in this room for days. There is a lot of time for both of us."

'Then he turned away and got undressed. He had a golden-brown body, a penis as smooth as the rest of his body, big, firm as a polished wood baton. She fell on him and took it into her mouth. His fingers went everywhere, into her anus, into her sex; his tongue, into her mouth, into her ears. He bit at her nipples, he kissed and bit her belly. She was trying to satisfy her hunger by rubbing against his leg, but he would not let her. He bent her as if she were made of rubber, twisted her into every position. With his two strong hands he took whatever part of her he was hungry for and brought it up to his mouth like a morsel of food, not caring how the rest of her body fell into space. Just so, he took her ass between his two hands, held it to his mouth, and bit and kissed her. She begged, "Take me, Antonio, take me, I can't wait!" He would not take her.

'By this time the hunger in her womb was like a raging fire. She thought that it would drive her insane. Whatever she tried to do to bring herself to an orgasm, he defeated. If she even kissed him too long he would break away. As she moved, the big belt made a clinking sound, like the chain of a slave. She was now indeed the slave of this enormous brown man. He ruled like a king. Her pleasure was subordinated to his. She realized she could do nothing against his force and will. He demanded submission. Her desire died in her from sheer exhaustion. All the tautness left her body. She became as soft as cotton. Into this he delved with greater exultancy. His slave, his possession, a broken body, panting, malleable, growing softer under his fingers. His hands searched every nook of her body, leaving nothing untouched, kneading it, kneading it to suit his fancy, bending it to suit his mouth, his tongue, pressing it against his big shining white teeth, marking her as his.

'For the first time, the hunger that had been on the surface of her skin like an irritation, retreated into a deeper part of her body. It retreated and accumulated, and it became a core of fire that waited to be exploded by his time and his rhythm. His touching was like a dance in which the bodies turned and deformed themselves into new shapes, new arrangements, new designs. Now they were cupped like twins, spoon-fashion, his penis against her ass, her breasts undulating like waves under his hands, painfully awake, aware, sensitive. Now he was crouching over her prone body like some great lion, as she placed her two fists under her ass to raise herself to his penis. He entered her for the first time and filled her as none other had, touching the very depths of the womb.

'The honey was pouring from her. As he pushed, his penis made little sucking sounds. All the air was drawn from the womb, the way his penis filled it, and he swung in and out of the honey endlessly, touching the tip of the womb, but as soon as her breathing hastened, he would draw it out, all glistening, and take up another form of caress. He lay back on the bed, legs apart, his penis raised, and he made her sit upon it, swallow it up to the hilt, so that her pubic hair rubbed against his. As he held her, he made her dance circles around his penis. She would fall on him and rub her breasts against his chest, and seek his mouth, then straighten up again and resume her motions around the penis. Sometimes she raised herself a little so that she kept only the head of the penis in her sex, and she moved lightly, very lightly, just enough to keep it inside, touching the edges of her sex, which were red and swollen, and clasped the penis like a mouth. Then suddenly moving downwards, engulfing the whole penis, and gasping with the joy, she would fall over his body and seek his mouth again. His hands remained on her ass all the time, gripping her to force her movements so that she could not suddenly accelerate them and come.

'He took her off the bed, laid her on the floor, on her hands and knees, and said, "Move." She began to crawl about the room, her long blond hair half-covering her, her belt weighing her waist down. Then he knelt behind her and inserted his penis, his whole body over hers, also moving on its iron knees and long arms. After he had enjoyed her from behind, he slipped his head under her so that he could suckle at her luxuriant breasts, as if she were an animal, holding her in place with his hands and mouth. They were both panting and twisting, and only then did he lift her up, carry her to the bed, and put her legs around his shoulders. He took her violently and they shook and trembled as they came together. She fell away suddenly and sobbed hysterically. The orgasm had been so strong that she had thought she would go insane, with a hatred and a joy like nothing she had ever known. He was smiling, panting they lay back and fell asleep.'

The next day Millard told me about the artist Mafouka, the man-woman of Montparnasse.

★

'No one knew exactly what she was. She dressed like a man. She was small, lean, flat-chested. She wore her hair short, straight. She had the face of a boy. She played billiards like a man. She drank like a man, with her foot on the bar railing. She told obscene stories like a man. Her drawing had a strength not found in a woman's work. But her name had a feminine sound, her walk was feminine, and she was said not to have a penis. The men did not know quite how to treat her. Sometimes they slapped her on the back with fraternal feelings.

'She lived with two girls in a studio. One of them was a model, the other, a nightclub singer. But no one knew what relationship there was among them. The two girls seemed to have a relationship like that of a husband and a wife. What was Mafouka to them? They would never answer any questions. Montparnasse always liked to know such things, and in detail. A few homosexuals had been attracted to Mafouka and had made advances toward her or him. But she had repulsed them. She quarreled willingly and struck out with force.

'One day I was quite a little drunk and I dropped into Mafouka's studio. The door was open. As I entered I heard giggling up on the balcony. The two girls were obviously making love. The voices would get soft and tender, then violent and unintelligible, and become moans and sighs. Then there would be silences.

'Mafouka came in and found me with my ear cocked, listening. I said to her, "Please let me go and see them."

'"I don't mind," said Mafouka. "Come up after me, slowly. They won't stop if they think it is just me. They like me to watch them."

'We went up the narrow stairs. Mafouka called, "It's I." There was no interruption of the noises. As we went up,

I bent over so that they could not see me. Mafouka went to the bed. The two girls were naked. They were pressing their bodies against each other and rubbing together. The friction gave them pleasure. Mafouka leaned over them, caressed them. They said, "Come on, Mafouka, lie with us." But she left them and took me downstairs again.

'"Mafouka," I said, "what are you? Are you a man or a woman? Why do you live with these two girls? If you are a man, why don't you have a girl of your own? If you are a woman, why don't you have a man occasionally?"

'Mafouka smiled at me.

'"Everybody wants to know. Everybody feels that I am not a boy. The women feel it. The men don't know for sure. I am an artist."

'"What do you mean, Mafouka?"

'"I mean that I am, like many artists, bisexual."

'"Yes, but the bisexuality of artists is in their nature. They may be a man with the nature of a woman, but with such an equivocal physique as you have."

'"I have an hermaphrodite's body."

'"Oh, Mafouka, let me see your body."

'"You won't make love to me?"

'"I promise."

'She took her shirt off first and showed a young boy's torso. She had no breasts, just the nipples, marked as they would be on a young boy. Then she slipped down her slacks. She was wearing a woman's panties, flesh-colored, with lace. She had a woman's legs and thighs. They were beautifully curved, full. She was wearing women's stockings and garters. I said, "Let me take the garters off. I love garters." She handed me her leg very elegantly with the movement of a ballet dancer. I slowly rolled down the garter. I held a dainty foot in my hand. I looked up

8

at her legs, which were perfect. I rolled down the stocking and saw beautiful, smooth, woman's skin. Her feet were dainty and carefully pedicured. Her nails were covered with red lacquer. I was more and more intrigued. I caressed her leg. She said, "You promised you would not make love to me."

'I stood up. Then she slipped down her panties. And I saw below the delicate curled pubic hair, shaped like a woman's, that she carried a small atrophied penis, like a child's. She let me look at her – or at him, as I felt I now should say.

'"Why do you call yourself by a woman's name, Mafouka? You are really like a young boy except for the shape of your legs and arms."

'Then Mafouka laughed, this time a woman's laugh, very light and pleasant. She said, "Come and see." She lay back on the couch, opened her legs and showed me a perfect vulva mouth, rosy and tender, behind the penis.

'"Mafouka!"

'My desire was aroused. The strangest desire. The feeling of wanting to take both a man and woman in one person. She saw the stirring of it in me and sat up. I tried to win her by a caress, but she eluded me.

'"Don't you like men?" I asked her. "Haven't you ever had a man?"

'"I'm a virgin. I don't like men. I feel a desire for women only, but I can't take them as a man could. My penis is like a child's – I cannot have an erection."

'"You are a real hermaphrodite, Mafouka," I said. "That is what our age is supposed to have produced because the tension between the masculine and the feminine has broken down. People are mostly half of one and half of the other. But I have never seen it before – actually, physically. It must make you very unhappy. Are you happy with women?"

"'I desire women, but I do suffer, because I cannot take them like a man, and also because when they have taken me like Lesbians, I still feel some dissatisfaction. But I am not attracted to men. I fell in love with Matilda, the model. But I could not keep her. She found a real Lesbian for herself, one that she feels she can satisfy. This penis of mine gives her the feeling that I am not a real Lesbian. And she knows she has no power over me, even though I was attracted to her. So you see, the two girls have formed another link together. I stand between them, perpetually dissatisfied. Also, I do not like the companionship of women. They are petty and personal. They hang on to their mysteries and secrets, they act and pretend. I like the character of men better."

"'Poor Mafouka.'"

"'Poor Mafouka. Yes, when I was born they did not know how to name me. I was born in a small village in Russia. They thought I was a monster and should perhaps be destroyed, for my own sake. When I came to Paris I suffered less. I found I was a good artist.'"

Whenever I left the sculptor's studio, I would always stop in a coffee shop nearby and ponder all that Millard had told me. I wondered whether anything like this were happening around me, here in Greenwich Village, for instance. I began to love posing, for the adventurous aspect of it. I decided to attend a party one Saturday evening that a painter named Brown had invited me to. I was hungry and curious about everything.

I rented an evening dress from the costume department of the Art Model Club, with an evening cape and shoes. Two of the models came with me, a red-haired girl, Mollie, and a statuesque one, Ethel, who was the favorite of the sculptors.

What was passing through my head all the time were the stories of Montparnasse life told to me by the sculptor, and now I felt that I was entering this realm. My first disappointment was seeing that the studio was quite poor and bare, the two couches without pillows, the lighting crude, with none of the trappings I had imagined necessary for a party.

Bottles were on the floor, along with glasses and chipped cups. A ladder led to a balcony where Brown kept his paintings. A thin curtain concealed the washstand and a little gas stove. At the front of the room was an erotic painting of a woman being possessed by two men. She was in a state of convulsion, her body arched, her eyes showing the whites. The men were covering her, one with his penis inside of her and the other with his penis in her mouth. It was a life-size painting and very bestial. Everyone was looking at it, admiring it. I was fascinated. It was the first picture of the sort I had seen, and it gave me a tremendous shock of mixed feelings.

Next to it stood another which was even more striking. It showed a poorly furnished room, filled by a big iron bed. Sitting on this bed was a man of about forty or so, in old clothes, with an unshaved face, a slobbering mouth, loose eyelids, loose jaws, a completely degenerate expression. He had taken his pants down halfway, and on his bare knees sat a little girl with very short skirts, to whom he was feeding a bar of candy. Her little bare legs rested on his bare hairy ones.

What I felt after seeing these two paintings was what one feels when drinking, a sudden dizziness of the head, a warmth through the body, a confusion of the senses.

Something awakens in the body, foggy and dim, a new sensation, a new kind of hunger and restlessness.

I looked at the other people in the room. But they had seen so much of this that it did not affect them. They laughed and commented.

One model was talking about her experiences at an underwear shop:

'I had answered an advertisement for a model to pose in underwear for sketches. I had done this many times before and was paid the normal price of a dollar an hour. Usually several artists sketched me at the same time, and there were many people around – secretaries, stenographers, errand boys. This time the place was empty. It was just an office with a desk, files and drawing materials. A man sat waiting for me in front of his drawing board. I was given a pile of underwear and found a screen placed where I could change. I began by wearing a slip. I posed for fifteen minutes at a time while he made sketches.

'We worked quietly. When he gave the signal, I went behind the screen and changed. They were satin under-things of lovely designs, with lace tops and fine embroidery. I wore a brassière and panties. The man smoked and sketched. At the bottom of the pile were panties and a brassière made entirely of black lace. I had posed in the nude often and did not mind wearing these. They were quite beautiful.

'I looked out of the window most of the time, not at the man sketching. After a while I did not hear the pencil working any longer and I turned slightly towards him, not wanting to lose the pose. He was sitting there behind his drawing board staring at me. Then I realized that he had his penis out and that he was in a kind of trance.

'Thinking this would mean trouble for me since we were alone in the office, I started to go behind the screen and dress.

'He said, "Don't go. I won't touch you. I just love to see women in lovely underwear. I won't move from here. And if you want me to pay you more, all you have to do is wear my favorite piece of underwear and pose for fifteen minutes. I will give you five dollars more. You can reach for it yourself. It is right above your head on the shelf there."

'Well, I did reach for the package. It was the loveliest piece of underwear you ever saw – the finest black lace, like a spider web really, and the panties were slit back and front, slit and edged with fine lace. The brassière was cut in such a way as to expose the nipples through triangles. I hesitated because I was wondering if this would not excite the man too much, if he would attack me.

'He said, "Don't worry. I don't really like women. I never touch them. I like only underwear. I just like to see women in lovely underwear. If I tried to touch you I would immediately become impotent. I won't move from here."

'He put aside the drawing board and sat there with his penis out. Now and then it shook. But he did not move from his chair.

'I decided to put on the underwear. The five dollars tempted me. He was not very strong and I felt that I could defend myself. So I stood there in the slit panties, turning around for him to see me on all sides.

'Then he said, "That's enough." He seemed unsettled and his face was congested. He told me to dress quickly and leave. He handed me the money in a great hurry, and I left. I had a feeling that he was only waiting for me to leave to masturbate.

'I have known men like this, who steal a shoe from someone, from an attractive woman, so they can hold it and masturbate while looking at it.'

Everyone was laughing at her story. 'I think,' said Brown, 'that when we are children we are much more inclined to be fetishists of one kind or another. I remember hiding inside my mother's closet and feeling ecstasy at smelling her clothes and feeling them. Even today I cannot resist a woman who is wearing a veil or tulle or feathers, because it awakens the strange feelings I had in that closet.'

As he said this I remembered how I hid in the closet of a young man when I was only thirteen, for the same reason. He was twenty-five and he treated me like a little girl. I was in love with him. Sitting next to him in a car in which he took all of us for long rides, I was ecstatic just feeling his leg alongside mine. At night I would get into bed and, after turning out the light, take out a can of condensed milk in which I had punctured a little hole. I would sit in the dark sucking at the sweet milk with a voluptuous feeling all over my body that I could not explain. I thought then that being in love and sucking at the sweet milk were related. Much later I remembered this when I tasted sperm for the first time.

Mollie remembered that at the same age she liked to eat ginger while she smelled camphor balls. The ginger made her body feel warm and languid and the camphor balls made her a little dizzy. She would get herself in a sort of drugged state this way, lying there for hours.

Ethel turned to me and said, 'I hope you never marry a man you don't love sexually. That is what I have done. I love everything about him, the way he behaves, his face, his body, the way he works, treats me, his thoughts, his way of smiling, talking, everything except the sexual man in him. I thought I did, before we married. There is absolutely nothing wrong with him. He is a perfect lover. He is emotional and romantic, he shows great feeling and great enjoyment. He is sensitive and adoring. Last night while I was asleep he came into my bed. I was half-asleep so I could not control myself, as I usually do, because I do not want to hurt his feelings. He got in beside me and began to take me very slowly and lingeringly. Usually it is all over quickly, which makes it possible to bear. I do not even let him kiss me if I can help it. I hate his mouth on mine. I usually turn my face away, which is what I did last night. Well, there he was, and what do you think I did? I suddenly began to strike him with my closed fists, on the shoulder, while he was enjoying himself, to dig my nails into him, and he took it as a sign that I was enjoying it, growing rather wild with pleasure, and he went on. Then I whispered as low as I could, "I hate you." And then I asked myself if he had heard me. What would he think? Was he hurt? As he was himself partly asleep, he merely kissed me good night when it was over and went back to his bed. The next morning I was waiting for what he would say. I still thought perhaps he had heard me say, "I hate you." But no, I must have formed the words without saying them. And all he said was, "You got quite wild last night, you know," and smiled, as if it pleased him.'

Brown started the phonograph and we began to dance. The little alcohol I had taken had gone to my head. I felt a dilation of the whole universe. Everything seemed very smooth and simple. Everything, in fact, ran downward like a snowy hill on which I could slide without effort. I felt a great friendliness, as if I knew all these people intimately. But I chose the most timid of the painters to dance with. I felt that he was pretending somewhat, as I was, to be very familiar with all of this. I felt that deep down he was a little uneasy. The other painters were caressing Ethel and Mollie as they danced. This one did not dare. I was laughing to myself at having discovered him. Brown saw that my painter was not making any advances, and he cut in for a dance. He was making sly remarks about virgins. I wondered whether he was alluding to me. How could he know? He pressed against me, and I drew away from him. I went back to the timid young painter. A woman illustrator was flirting with him, teasing him. He was equally glad that I came back to him. So we danced together, retreating into our own timidity. All around us people were kissing now, embracing.

The woman illustrator had thrown off her blouse and was dancing in her slip. The timid painter said, 'If we stay here we will soon have to lie on the floor and make love. Do you want to leave?'

'Yes, I want to leave,' I said.

We went out. Instead of making love, he was talking, talking. I was listening to him in a daze. He had a plan for a picture of me. He wanted to paint me as an undersea woman, nebulous, transparent, green, watery except for the very red mouth and the very red flower I was wearing in my hair. Would I pose for him? I did not respond very quickly because of the effects of the liquor, and he said apologetically, 'Are you sorry that I was not brutal?'

'No, I'm not sorry. I chose you myself because I knew you would not be.'

'It's my first party,' he said humbly, 'and you're not the kind of woman one can treat – that way. How did you ever become a model? What did you do before this? A model does not have to be a prostitute, I know, but she has to bear a lot of handling and attempts.'

'I manage quite well,' I said, not enjoying this conversation at all.

'I will be worrying about you. I know some artists are objective while they work, I know all that. I feel that way myself. But there is always a moment before and after, when the model is undressing and dressing, that does disturb me. It's the first surprise of seeing the body. What did you feel the first time?'

'Nothing at all. I felt as if I were a painting already. Or a statue. I looked down at my own body like some object, some impersonal object.'

I was growing sad, sad with restlessness and hunger. I felt that nothing would happen to me. I felt desperate with desire to be a woman, to plunge into living. Why was I enslaved by this need of being in love first? Where would my life begin? I would enter each studio expecting a miracle which did not take place. It seemed to me that a great current was passing all around me and that I was left out. I would have to find someone who felt as I did. But where? Where?

The sculptor was watched by his wife, I could see that. She came into the studio so often, unexpectedly. And he was frightened. I did not know what frightened him. They invited me to spend two weeks at their country house where I would continue to pose – or rather, she invited me. She said that her husband did not like to stop work during vacations. But as soon as she left he turned to me and said, 'You must find an excuse not to go. She will make you miserable. She is not well – she has obsessions. She thinks that every woman who poses for me is my mistress.'

There were hectic days of running from studio to studio with very little time for lunch, posing for magazine covers, illustrations for magazine stories, and advertisements. I could see my face everywhere, even in the subway. I wondered if people recognized me.

The sculptor had become my best friend. I was anxiously watching his statuette coming to a finish. Then one morning when I arrived I saw that he had ruined it. He said that he had tried to work on it without me. But he did not seem unhappy or worried. I was quite sad, and to me it looked very much like sabotage, because it seemed spoiled with such awkwardness. I saw that he was happy to be beginning it all over again.

It was at the theater that I met John and discovered the power of a voice. It rolled over me like the tones of a pipe organ, making me vibrate. When he repeated my name and mispronounced it, it sounded to me like a caress. It was the deepest, richest voice I had ever heard. I could scarcely look at him. I knew that his eyes were big, of an intense, magnetic blue, that he was large, rather restless. His foot moved nervously like that of a racehorse. I felt his presence blurring everything else – the theater, the friend sitting at my right. And he behaved as if I had enchanted him, hypnotized him. He talked on, looking at me, but I was not listening. In one moment I was no longer a young girl. Every time he spoke, I felt myself falling into some dizzy spiral, falling into the meshes of a beautiful voice. It was truly a drug. When he had finally 'stolen' me, as he said, he hailed a taxi.

We did not say another word until we reached his apartment. He had not touched me. He did not need to. His presence had affected me in such a way that I felt as if he had caressed me for a long time.

He merely said my name twice, as if he thought it sufficiently beautiful to repeat. He was tall, glowing. His eyes were so intensely blue that when they blinked, for a second it was like some tiny flash of lightning, giving one a sense of fear, a fear of a storm that would completely engulf one.

Then he kissed me. His tongue went around mine, around and around, and then it stopped to touch the tip only. As he kissed me he slowly lifted my skirt. He unrolled my garters, my stockings. Then he lifted me up and carried me to the bed. I was so dissolved that I felt he had already penetrated me. It seemed to me that his voice had opened me, opened my whole body to him. He sensed this, and so he was amazed by the resistance to his penis that he felt.

He stopped to look at my face. He saw the great emotional receptiveness, and then he pressed harder. I felt the tear and the pain, but the warmth melted everything, the warmth of his voice in my ear saying, 'Do you want me as I want you?'

Then his pleasure made him groan. His whole weight upon me, pressing against my body, the shaft of pain vanished. I felt the joy of being opened. I lay there in a semidream.

John said, 'I hurt you. You did not enjoy it.' I could not say, 'I want it again.' My hand touched his penis. I caressed it. It sprung up, so hard. He kissed me until I felt a new wave of desire, a desire to respond completely. But he said, 'It will hurt now. Wait a little while. Can you stay with me, all night? Will you stay?'

I saw that there was blood on my leg. I went to wash it off. I felt that I had not been taken yet, that this was only a small part of the breaking through. I wanted to be possessed and know blinding joys. I walked unsteadily and fell on the bed again.

John was asleep, his big body still curved as when he

was lying against me, his arm thrown out where my head had been resting. I slipped in at his side and fell half-asleep. I wanted to touch his penis again. I did so gently, not wanting to wake him. Then I slept and was awakened by his kisses. We were floating in a dark world of flesh, feeling only the soft flesh vibrating, and every touch was a joy. He gripped my hips tautly against him. He was afraid to wound me. I parted my legs. When he inserted his penis it hurt, but the pleasure was greater. There was a little outer rim of pain and, deeper in, a pleasure at the presence of his penis moving there. I pressed forwards, to meet it.

This time he was passive. He said, 'You move, you enjoy it now.' So as not to feel the pain, I moved gently around his penis. I put my closed fists under my backside to raise myself toward him. He placed my legs on his shoulders. Then the pain grew greater and he withdrew.

I left him in the morning, dazed, but with a new joy of feeling that I was growing nearer to passion. I went home and slept until he telephoned.

'When are you coming?' he said. 'I must see you again. Soon. Are you posing today?'

'Yes, I must. I'll come after the pose.'

'Please don't pose,' he said, 'please don't pose. It makes me desperate to think of it. Come and see me first. I want to talk to you. Please come and see me first.'

I went to him. 'Oh,' he said, burning my face with the breath of his desire. 'I can't bear to think of you posing now, exposing yourself. You can't do that anymore. You must let me take care of you. I cannot marry you because I have a wife and children. Let me take care of you until we know how we can escape. Let me get a little place where I can come and see you. You should not be posing. You belong to me.'

So I entered a secret life, and when I was supposed to be posing for everyone else in the world, I was really waiting in a beautiful room for John. Each time he came, he brought a gift, a book, colored stationery for me to write on. I was restless, waiting.

The only one who was taken into the secret was the sculptor because he sensed what was happening. He would not let me stop posing, and he questioned me. He had predicted how my life would be.

The first time I felt an orgasm with John, I wept because it was so strong and so marvelous that I did not believe it could happen over and over again. The only painful moments were the ones spent waiting. I would bathe myself, spread polish on my nails, perfume myself, rouge my nipples, brush my hair, put on a negligée, and all the preparations would turn my imagination to the scenes to come.

I wanted him to find me in the bath. He would say he was on his way. But he would not arrive. He was often detained. By the time he arrived I would be cold, resentful. The waiting wore out my feelings. I would rebel. Once I would not answer when he rang the doorbell. Then he knocked gently, humbly, and that touched me, so I opened the door. But I was angry and wanted to hurt him. I did not respond to his kiss. He was hurt until his hand slipped under my negligée and he found that I was wet, in spite of the fact that I kept my legs tightly closed. He was joyous again and he forced his way.

Then I punished him by not responding sexually and he was hurt again, for he enjoyed my pleasure. He knew by the violent heartbeats, by the changes in the voice, by the contraction of my legs, how I had enjoyed him. And this time I lay like a whore. That really hurt him.

We could never go out together. He was too well known, as was his wife. He was a producer. His wife was a playwright.

When John discovered how angry it would make me to wait for him, he did not try to remedy it. He came later and later. He would say that he was arriving at ten o'clock and then come at midnight. So one day he found that I was not there when he came. This put him in a frenzy. He thought I would not come back. I felt that he was doing this deliberately, that he liked my being angry. After two days he pleaded with me and I returned. We were both very keyed up and angry.

He said, 'You've gone back to pose. You like it. You like to show yourself.'

'Why do you make me wait so long? You know that it kills my desire for you. I feel cold when you come late.'

'Not so very cold,' he said.

I closed my legs tightly against him, he could not even touch me. But then he slipped in quickly from behind and caressed me. 'Not so cold,' he said.

On the bed he pushed his knee between my legs and forced them open. 'When you are angry,' he said, 'I feel that I am raping you. I feel then that you love me so much you cannot resist me, I see that you are wet, and I like your resistance and your defeat too.'

'John, you will make me so angry that I will leave you.'

Then he was frightened. He kissed me. He promised not to repeat this.

What I could not understand was that, despite our quarrels, being made love to by John made me only more sensitive. He had awakened my body. Now I had even a greater desire to abandon myself to all whims. He must have known this because the more he caressed me, awakened me, the more he feared that I would return to posing. Slowly, I did return. I had too much time to myself, I was too much alone with my thoughts of John.

Millard particularly was happy to see me. He must have spoiled the statuette again, purposely I knew now, so he could keep me in the pose he liked.

The night before, he had smoked marijuana with friends. He said, 'Did you know that very often it gives people the feeling that they are transformed into animals? Last night there was a woman who was completely taken by this transformation. She fell on her hands and knees and walked around like a dog. We took her clothes off. She wanted to give milk. She wanted us to act like puppies, sprawl on the floor and suckle at her breasts. She kept on her hands and knees and offered her breasts to all of us. She wanted us to walk like dogs – after her. She insisted on our taking her in this position, from behind, and I did, but then I was terribly tempted to bite her as I crouched over her. I bit into her shoulder harder than I have ever bitten anyone. The woman did not get frightened. I did. It sobered me. I stood up and then saw that a friend of mine was following her on his hands and knees, not caressing her or taking her, but merely smelling exactly as a dog would do, and this reminded me so much of my first sexual impression that it gave me a painful hard-on.

'As children we had a big servant girl in the country who came from Martinique. She wore voluminous skirts and a colored kerchief on her head. She was a rather pale mulatto, very beautiful. She would make us play hide-and-seek. When it was my turn to hide she would hide me under her skirt, sitting down. And there I was, half-suffocated, hiding between her legs. I remember the sexual odor that came from her and that stirred me even as a boy. Once I tried to touch her, but she slapped my hand.'

I was posing quietly and he came over to measure me with an instrument. Then I felt his hand on my thighs, caressing me so lightly. I smiled at him. I stood on the model's stand, and he was caressing my legs now, as if he were modeling me out of clay. He kissed my feet, he ran his hands up my legs again and again, and around my ass. He leaned against my legs and kissed me. He lifted me up and brought me down to the floor. He held me tightly against him, caressing my back and shoulders and neck. I shivered a little. His hands were smooth and supple. He touched me as he touched the statuette, so caressingly, all over.

Then we walked towards the couch. He lay me there on my stomach. He took his clothes off and fell on me. I felt his penis against my ass. He slipped his hands around my waist and lifted me up slightly so that he could penetrate me. He lifted me up toward him rhythmically. I closed my eyes to feel him better and to listen to the sound of the penis sliding in and out of the moisture. He pushed so violently that it made tiny clicks, which delighted me.

His fingers dug into my flesh. His nails were sharp and hurt. He aroused me so much with his vigorous thrusts that my mouth opened and I was biting into the couch cover. Then at the same time we both heard a sound. Millard rose swiftly, picked up his clothes and ran up the ladder to the balcony where he kept his sculpture. I slipped behind the screen.

There came a second knock on the studio door, and his wife came in. I was trembling, not with fear, but the shock of having stopped in the middle of our enjoyment. Millard's wife saw the studio empty and left. Millard came out dressed. I said, 'Wait for me a minute,' and began to dress too. The moment was destroyed. I was still wet and shivering. When I slipped on my panties the silk touch affected me like a hand. I could not bear the tension and desire any longer. I put my two hands over my sex as Millard had done and pressed against it, closing my eyes and imagining Millard was caressing me. And I came, shaking from head to foot.

Millard wanted to be with me again, but not in his studio where we might be surprised by his wife, so I let him find another place. It belonged to a friend. The bed was set in a deep alcove and there were mirrors above the bed and small dim lamps. Millard wanted all the lights out, he said he wanted to be in the dark with me.

'I have seen your body and I know it so well, now I want to feel it, with my eyes closed, just to feel the skin and the softness of the flesh. Your legs are so firm and strong, but so soft to the touch. I love your feet with the toes free and set apart like the fingers of a hand, not cramped – and the toenails so beautifully lacquered – and the down on your legs.' He passed his hand all over my body, slowly, pressing into the flesh, feeling every curve. 'If my hand stays here between the legs,' he said, 'do you feel it, do you like it, do you want it nearer?'

'Nearer, nearer,' I said.

'I want to teach you something,' said Millard. 'Do you want to let me do it?'

He inserted his finger inside my sex. 'Now, I want you to contract around my finger. There is a muscle there that can be made to contract and expand around the penis. Try.'

I tried. His finger there was tantalizing. Since he was not moving it, I tried to move inside of my womb, and I felt the muscle that he mentioned, weakly at first, opening and closing around the finger.

Millard said, 'Yes, like that. Do it stronger, stronger.'

So I did, opening, closing, opening, closing. It was like a little mouth inside, tightening around the finger. I wanted to take it in, suckle at it, so I continued to try.

Then Millard said that he would insert his penis and not move and that I should continue to move inside. I tried with more and more strength to clutch at him. The motion was exciting me, and I felt that at any moment I would reach the orgasm, but after I had clutched at him several times, sucking his penis in, he suddenly groaned with pleasure and began to push quickly, as he himself could not hold back the orgasm. I merely continued the inner motion and I felt the orgasm, too, in the most marvelous deep way, deep inside of the womb.

He said, 'Did John ever show you this?'

'No.'

'What has he shown you?'

'This,' I said. 'You kneel over me and push.'

Millard obeyed. His penis did not have much strength, for it was too soon after the first orgasm, but he slipped it in, pushing it with his hand. Then I reached out with my two hands and caressed the balls and put two fingers at the base of the penis and rubbed as he moved. Millard was instantly aroused, his penis hardened, and he began to move in and out again. Then he stopped himself.

'I must not be so demanding,' he said in a strange tone. 'You will be tired out for John.'

We lay back and rested, smoking. I was wondering if Millard had felt more than sensual desire, whether my love for John weighed on him. But although there was always a hurt sound to his words, he continued to ask me questions.

'Did John have you today? Did he take you more than once? How did he take you?'

In the weeks to come, Millard taught me many things I had not done with John, and as soon as I learned them I tried them with John. Finally he became suspicious of where I was learning new positions. He knew I had not made love before I met him. The first time I tightened my muscles to clutch at the penis, he was amazed.

The two secret relationships became difficult for me, but I enjoyed the danger and the intensity.

A Model

My mother had European ideas about young girls. I was
sixteen. I had never gone out alone with young men, I had
never read anything but literary novels, and by choice I
never was like girls my own age. I was what you would
call a sheltered person, very much like some Chinese
woman, instructed in the art of making the most of the
discarded dresses sent to me by a rich cousin, singing and
dancing, writing elegantly, reading the finest books,
conversing intelligently, arranging my hair beautifully,
keeping my hands white and delicate, using only the
refined English I had learned since my arrival from France,
dealing with everybody in terms of great politeness.

This was what was left of my European education. But
I was very much like the Orientals in one other way: long
periods of gentleness were followed by bursts of violence,
taking the form of temper and rebellion or of quick decision and positive action.

I suddenly decided to go to work, without consulting
anybody or asking anybody's approval. I knew my mother
would be against my plan.

I had rarely gone to New York alone. Now I walked
the streets, answering all kinds of advertisements. My
accomplishments were not very practical. I knew
languages but not typewriting. I knew Spanish dancing
but not the new ballroom dances. Everywhere I went I
did not inspire confidence. I looked even younger than
my age and over-delicate, over-sensitive. I looked as if I

could not bear any burdens put on me, yet this was only an appearance.

After a week I had obtained nothing but a sense of not being useful to anyone. It was then I went to see a family friend who was very fond of me. She had disapproved of my mother's way of protecting me. She was happy to see me, amazed at my decision and willing to help me. It was while talking to her humorously about myself, enumerating my assets, that I happened to say that a painter had come to see us the week before and had said that I had an exotic face. My friend jumped up.

'I have it,' she said. 'I know what you can do. It is true that you have an unusual face. Now I know an art club where artists go for their models. I will introduce you there. It is a sort of protection for the girls, instead of having them walk about from studio to studio. The artists are registered at the club, where they are known, and they telephone when they need a model.'

When we arrived at the club on Fifty-seventh Street, there was great animation and many people. It turned out that they were preparing for the annual show. Every year all the models were dressed in costumes that best suited them and exhibited to the painters. I was quickly registered for a small fee and was sent upstairs to two elderly ladies who took me into the costume room. One of them chose an eighteenth-century costume. The other fixed my hair above my ears. They taught me how to wax my eyelashes. I saw a new self in the mirrors. The rehearsal was going on. I had to walk downstairs and stroll around the room. It was not difficult. It was like a masquerade ball.

The day of the show everyone was rather nervous. Much of a model's success depended on this event. My hand trembled as I made up my eyelashes. I was given a rose to carry, which made me feel a little ridiculous. I was received with applause. After all the girls had walked slowly around the room, the painters talked with us, took down our names, made engagements. My engagement book was filled like a dance card.

Monday at nine o'clock I was to be at the studio of a well-known painter; at one, at the studio of an illustrator; at four, at the studio of a miniaturist, and so on. There were women painters too. They objected to our using make-up. They said that when they engaged a made-up model and then got her to wash her face before posing, she did not look the same. For that reason posing for women did not attract us very much.

My announcement at home that I was a model came like a thunderbolt. But it was done. I could make twenty-five dollars a week. My mother wept a little, but was pleased deep down.

That night we talked in the dark. Her room connected with mine and the door was open. My mother was worrying about what I knew (or did not know) about sex.

The sum of my knowledge was this: that I had been kissed many times by Stephen, lying on the sand at the beach. He had been lying over me, and I had felt something bulky and hard pressing against me, but that was all, and to my great amazement when I came home I had discovered that I was all wet between the legs. I had not mentioned this to my mother. My private impression was that I was a great sensualist, that this getting wet between the legs at being kissed showed dangerous tendencies for the future. In fact, I felt quite like a whore.

My mother asked me, 'Do you know what happens when a man takes a woman?'

'No,' I said, 'but I would like to know *how* a man takes a woman in the first place.'

'Well, you know the small penis you saw when you bathed your brother – that gets big and hard and the man pushes it inside of the woman.'

That seemed ugly to me. 'It must be difficult to get it in,' I said.

'No, because the woman gets wet before that, so it slides in easily.'

Now I understood the mystery of wetness.

In that case, I thought to myself, I will never get raped, because to get wet you have to like the man.

A few months before, having been violently kissed in the woods by a big Russian who was bringing me home from a dance, I had come home and announced that I was pregnant.

Now I remembered how one night when several of us were returning from another dance, driving along the speedway, we had heard girls screaming. My escort, John, stopped the car. Two girls ran to us from the bushes, disheveled, dresses torn and eyes haggard. We let them into the car. They were mumbling chaotically about having been taken for a ride on a motorcycle and then attacked. One of them kept saying: 'If he broke through, I'll kill myself.'

John stopped at an inn and I took the girls to the ladies' room. They immediately went into the toilet together. One was saying: 'There is no blood. I guess he didn't break through.' The other one was crying.

We took them home. One of the girls thanked me and said, 'I hope that never happens to you.'

While my mother was talking, I was wondering if she feared this and was preparing me.

I cannot say that when Monday came I was not uneasy. I felt that if the painter was attractive I would be in greater danger than if he was not, for if I liked him I might get wet between the legs.

The first one was about fifty, bald, with a rather European face and a little mustache. He had a beautiful studio.

He placed the screen in front of me so that I could change my dress. I threw my clothes over the screen. As I threw my last piece of underwear over the top of the screen, I saw the painter's face appear at the top, smiling. But it was done so comically and ridiculously, like a scene in a play, that I said nothing, got dressed and took the pose.

Every half-hour I would get a rest. I could smoke a cigarette. The painter put on a record and said: 'Will you dance?'

We danced on the highly polished floor, turning among the paintings of beautiful women. At the end of the dance, he kissed my neck. 'So dainty,' he said. 'Do you pose in the nude?'

'No.'

'Too bad.'

I thought this was not so difficult to manage. It was time to pose again. The three hours passed quickly. He talked while he worked. He said he had married his first model; that she was unbearably jealous; that every now and then she broke into the studio and made scenes; that she would not let him paint from the nude. He had rented another studio she did not know about. Often he worked there. He gave parties there too. Would I like to come to one on Saturday night?

He gave me another little kiss on the neck as I left. He winked and said: 'You won't tell the club on me?'

I returned to the club for luncheon because I could make up my face and freshen myself, and they gave us a cheap lunch. The other girls were there. We fell into conversation. When I mentioned the invitation for Saturday night, they laughed, nodding at one another. I could not get them to talk. One girl had lifted up her skirt and was examining a mole way up her thighs. With a little caustic pencil she was trying to burn it away. I saw that she was not wearing panties, just a black satin dress which clung to her. The telephone would ring and then one of the girls would be called and go off to work.

The next was a young illustrator. He was wearing his shirt open at the neck. He did not move when I came in. He shouted at me, 'I want to see a lot of back and shoulders. Put a shawl around yourself or something.' Then he gave me a small old-fashioned umbrella and white gloves. The shawl he pinned down almost to my waist. This was for a magazine cover.

The arrangement of the shawl over my breasts was precarious. As I tilted my head at the angle he wanted, in a sort of inviting gesture, the shawl slipped and my breasts showed. He would not let me move. 'Wish I could paint them in,' he said.

He was smiling as he worked with his charcoal pencil. Leaning over to measure me, he touched the tips of my breasts with his pencil and made a little black mark. 'Keep that pose,' he said as he saw me ready to move. I kept it.

Then he said: 'You girls sometimes act as if you thought you were the only ones with breasts or asses. I see so many of them they don't interest me, I assure you. I take my wife all dressed always. The more clothes she has on the better. I turn off the light. I know too much how women are made. I've drawn millions of them.'

The little touch of the pencil on my breasts had hardened the tips. This angered me, because I had not felt it a pleasure at all. Why were my breasts so sensitive, and did he notice it?

He went on drawing and coloring his picture. He stopped to drink whiskey and offered me some. He dipped his finger in the whiskey and touched one of my nipples. I was not posing so I moved away angrily. He kept smiling at me. 'Doesn't it feel nice?' he said. 'It warms them.'

It was true that the tips were hard and red.

'Very nice nipples you have. You don't need to use lipstick on them, do you? They are naturally rosy. Most of them have a leather color.'

I covered myself.

That was all for that day. He asked me to come the next day at the same time.

He was slower in getting to his work on Tuesday. He talked. He had his feet up on his drawing table. He offered me a cigarette. I was pinning up my shawl. He was watching me. He said: 'Show me your legs. I may do a drawing of legs next time.'

I lifted up my skirt above the knee.

'Sit down with your skirt up high,' he said.

He sketched in the legs. There was a silence.

Then he got up, flung his pencil on the table, leaned over me and kissed me fully on the mouth, forcing my head backwards. I pushed him off violently. This made him smile. He slipped his hand swiftly up under my skirt, felt my thighs where the stockings stopped and before I could move was back in his seat.

I took the pose and said nothing, because I had just made a discovery – that in spite of my anger, in spite of the fact that I was not in love, the kiss and the caress on the naked thighs had given me pleasure. While I fought him off, it was only out of habit, but actually it had given me pleasure.

The pose gave me time to awaken from the pleasure and remember my defenses. But my defenses had been convincing and he was quiet for the rest of the morning.

From the very first I had divined that what I really had to defend myself against was my own susceptibility to caresses. I was also filled with great curiosities about so many things. At the same time I was utterly convinced that I would not give myself to anyone but the man I fell in love with.

I was in love with Stephen. I wanted to go to him and say: 'Take me, take me!' I suddenly remembered another incident, and that was a year before this when one of my aunts had taken me to New Orleans to the Mardi Gras. Friends of hers had driven us in their automobile. There were two other young girls with us. A band of young men took advantage of the confusion, the noise, the excitement and gaiety to jump into our automobile, remove our masks and begin kissing us while my aunt raised an outcry. Then they disappeared into the crowd. I was left dazed and wishing that the young man who had taken hold of me and had kissed me on the mouth were still there. I was languid from the kiss, languid and stirred.

Back at the club I wondered what all the rest of the models felt. There was a great deal of talk about defending oneself, and I wondered whether it was all sincere. One of the loveliest models, whose face was not particularly beautiful but who had a magnificent body, was talking:

'I don't know what other girls feel about posing in the nude,' she said, 'I love it. Ever since I was a little girl I liked taking off my clothes. I liked to see how people looked at me. I used to take my clothes off at parties, as soon as people were a little drunk. I liked showing my body. Now I can't wait to take them off. I enjoy being looked at. It gives me pleasure. I get shivers of pleasure right down my back when men look at me. And when I pose for a whole class of artists at the school, when I see all those eyes on my body, I get so much pleasure, it is – well, it is like being made love to. I feel beautiful, I feel as women must feel sometimes when undressed for a lover. I enjoy my own body. I like to pose holding my breasts in my hand. Sometimes I caress them. I was once in burlesque. I loved it. I enjoyed doing that as much as the men enjoyed seeing it. The satin of the dress used to give me shivers – taking my breasts out, exposing myself. That excited me. When men touched me I did not get as much excitement . . . it was always a disappointment. But I know other girls who don't feel that way.'

'I feel humiliated,' said a red-haired model. 'I feel my body is not my own, and that it no longer has any value . . . being seen by everybody.'

'I don't feel anything at all,' said another. 'I feel it's all impersonal. When men are painting or drawing, they no longer think of us as human beings. One painter told me that the body of a model on the stand is an objective thing, that the only moment he felt disturbed erotically was when the model took off her kimono. In Paris, they tell me, the model undresses right in front of the class, and that's exciting.'

'If it were all so objective,' said another girl, 'they wouldn't invite us to parties afterwards.'

'Or marry their models,' I added, remembering two painters I had already met who had married their favorite models.

*

A Model

One day I had to pose for an illustrator of stories. When I arrived, I found two other people already there, a girl and a man. We were to compose scenes together, love scenes for a romance. The man was about forty, with a very mature, very decadent face. It was he who knew how to arrange us. He placed me in a position for a kiss. We had to hold the pose while the illustrator photographed us. I was uneasy. I did not like the man at all. The other girl played the jealous wife who burst in on the scene. We had to do it many times. Each time the man acted the kiss I shrank inside myself, and he felt it. He was offended. His eyes were mocking. I acted badly. The illustrator was shouting at me as if we were in a moving picture, 'More passion, put more passion into it!'

I tried to remember how the Russian had kissed me on returning from the dance, and that relaxed me. The man repeated the kiss. And now I felt he was holding me closer than he needed to, and surely he did not need to push his tongue into my mouth. He did it so quickly that I had no time to move. The illustrator started other scenes.

The male model said, 'I have been a model for ten years now. I don't know why they always want young girls. Young girls have no experience and no expression. In Europe young girls of your age, under twenty, do not interest anyone. They are left in school or at home. They only become interesting after marriage.'

As he talked, I thought of Stephen. I thought of us at the beach, lying on the hot sand. I knew that Stephen loved me. I wanted him to take me. I wanted now to be made a woman quickly. I did not like being a virgin, always defending myself. I felt that everyone knew I was a virgin and was all the more keen to conquer me.

That evening Stephen and I were going out together. Somehow or other I must tell him. I must tell him that I was in danger of being raped, that he'd better do it first. No, he would then be so anxious. How could I tell him?

I had news for him. I was the star model now. I had more work than anyone else in the club, there were more demands for me because I was a foreigner and had an unusual face. I often had to pose in the evenings. I told Stephen all this. He was proud of me.

'You like your posing?' he said.

'I love it. I love to be with painters, to see them work – good or bad, I like the atmosphere of it, the stories I hear. It is varied, never the same. It is really adventure.'

'Do they . . . do they make love to you?' Stephen asked.

'Not if you don't want them to.'

'But do they try . . . ?'

I saw that he was anxious. We were walking to my house from the railway station, through the dark fields. I turned to him and offered my mouth. He kissed me. I said, 'Stephen, take me, take me, take me.'

He was completely dumbfounded. I was throwing myself into the refuge of his big arms, I wanted to be taken and have it all over with, I wanted to be made woman. But he was absolutely still, frightened. He said, 'I want to marry you, but I can't do it just now.'

'I don't care about the marriage.'

But now I became conscious of his surprise, and it quieted me. I was immensely disappointed by his conventional attitude. The moment passed. He thought it was merely an attack of blind passion, that I had lost my head. He was even proud to have protected me against my own impulses. I went home to bed and sobbed.

One illustrator asked me if I would pose on Sunday, that he was in a great rush to finish a poster. I consented. When

I arrived he was already at work. It was morning and the building seemed deserted. His studio was on the thirteenth floor. He had half of the poster done. I got undressed quickly and put on the evening dress he had given me to wear. He did not seem to pay any attention to me. We worked in peace for a long while. I grew tired. He noticed it and gave me a rest. I walked about the studio looking at the other pictures. They were mostly portraits of actresses. I asked him who they were. He answered me with details about their sexual tastes:

'Oh, this one, this one demands romanticism. It's the only way you can get near her. She makes it difficult. She is European and she likes an intricate courtship. Halfway through I gave it up. It was too strenuous. She was very beautiful though, and there is something wonderful about getting a woman like that in bed. She had beautiful eyes, an entranced air, like some Hindu mystic. It makes you wonder how they will behave in bed.

'I have known other sexual angels. It is wonderful to see the change in them. These clear eyes that you can see through, these bodies that take such beautiful harmonious poses, these delicate hands . . . how they change when desire takes hold of them. The sexual angels! They are wonderful because it is such a surprise, such a change. You, for instance, with your appearance of never having been touched, I can see you biting and scratching . . . I am sure your very voice changes – I have seen such changes. There are women's voices that sound like poetic, unearthly echoes. Then they change. The eyes change. I believe that all these legends about people changing into animals at night – like the stories of the werewolf, for instance – were invented by men who saw women transform at night from idealized, worshipful creatures into animals and thought that they were possessed. But I know it is something much simpler than that. You are a virgin, aren't you?'

'No, I am married,' I said.

'Married or not, you are a virgin. I can tell. I am never deceived. If you are married, your husband has not made you a woman yet. Don't you regret that? Don't you feel you are wasting time, that real living begins with sensation, with being a woman . . . ?'

This corresponded so exactly to what I had been feeling, to my desire to enter experience, that I was silent. I hated to admit this to a stranger.

I was conscious of being alone with the illustrator in an empty studio building. I was sad that Stephen had not understood my desire to become a woman. I was not frightened but fatalistic, desiring only to find someone I might fall in love with.

'I know what you are thinking,' he said, 'but for me it would not have any meaning unless the woman wanted me. I never could make love to a woman if she did not want me. When I first saw you, I felt how wonderful it would be to initiate you. There is something about you that makes me feel you will have many love affairs. I would like to be the first one. But not unless you wanted it.'

I smiled. 'That is exactly what I was thinking. It can only be if I want it, and I do not want it.'

'You must not give that first surrender so much importance. I think that was created by the people who wanted to preserve their daughters for marriage, the idea that the first man who takes a woman will have complete power over her. I think that is a superstition. It was created to help preserve women from promiscuity. It is actually untrue. If a man can make himself be loved, if he can rouse a woman, then she will be attracted to him. But the mere act of breaking through her virginity is not enough to accomplish this. Any man can do this and leave the woman unaroused. Did you know that many Spaniards take their wives this way and give them many children without completely initiating them sexually just to be sure of their faithfulness? The Spaniard believes in keeping pleasure for his mistress. In fact, if he sees a woman enjoy sensuality, he immediately suspects her of being faithless, even of being a whore.'

The illustrator's words haunted me for days. Then I was faced with a new problem. Summer had come and the painters were leaving for the country, for the beach, for far-off places in all directions. I did not have the money to follow them, and I was not sure how much work I would get. One morning I posed for an illustrator named Ronald. Afterwards he set the phonograph going and asked me to dance. While we were dancing he said, 'Why don't you come to the country for a while? It will do you good, you will get plenty of work, and I will pay for your trip. There are very few good models there. I am sure you will be kept busy.'

So I went. I took a little room in a farmhouse. Then I went to see Ronald, who lived down the road in a shed, into which he had built a huge window. The first thing he did was to blow his cigarette smoke into my mouth. I coughed.

'Oh,' he said, 'you don't know how to inhale.'

'I'm not at all interested,' I said, getting up. 'What kind of pose do you want?'

'Oh,' he said laughing, 'We don't work so hard here. You will have to learn to enjoy yourself a little. Now, take the smoke from my mouth and inhale it . . .'

'I don't like to inhale.'

He laughed again. He tried to kiss me. I moved away.

'Oh, oh,' he said, 'you are not going to be a very pleasant companion for me. I paid for your trip, you know, and I'm lonely down here. I expected you to be very pleasant company. Where is your suitcase?'

'I took a room down the road.'

'But you were invited to stay with me,' he said.

'I understood you wanted me to pose for you.'

'For the moment it is not a model I need.'

I started to leave. He said, 'You know, there is an understanding here about models who do not know how to enjoy themselves. If you take this attitude nobody will give you any work.'

I did not believe him. The next morning I began to knock on the doors of all the artists I could find. But Ronald had already paid them a visit. So I was received without cordiality, like a person who has played a trick on another. I did not have the money to return home, nor the money to pay for my room. I knew nobody. The country was beautiful, mountainous, but I could not enjoy it.

The next day I took a long walk and came upon a log cabin by the side of a river. I saw a man painting there, out of doors. I spoke to him. I told him my story. He did not know Ronald, but he was angry. He said he would try to help me. I told him all I wanted was to earn enough to return to New York.

So I began to pose for him. His name was Reynolds. He was a man of thirty or so, with black hair, very soft black eyes and a brilliant smile – a recluse. He never went to the village, except for food, nor frequented the restaurants or bars. He had a lax walk, easy gestures. He had been on the sea, always on tramp steamers, working as a sailor so that he could see foreign countries. He was always restless.

He painted from memory what he had seen in his travels. Now he sat at the foot of a tree and never looked around him but painted a wild piece of South American jungle.

Once when he and his friends were in the jungle, Reynolds told me, they had smelled such a strong animal odor they thought they would suddenly see a panther, but out of the bushes had sprung with incredible velocity a woman, a naked savage woman, who looked at them with the frightened eyes of an animal, then ran off, leaving this strong animal scent behind her, threw herself into the river and swam away before they could catch their breath.

A friend of Reynolds had captured a woman like this. When he had washed off the red paint with which she was covered, she was very beautiful. She was gentle when well treated, succumbed to gifts of beads and ornaments.

Her strong smell repelled Reynolds until his friend had offered to let him have a night with her. He had found her black hair as hard and bristly as a beard. The animal smell made him feel he was lying with a panther. And she was so much stronger than he that after a while, he was acting almost like a woman, and she was the one who was molding him to suit her fancies. She was indefatigable and slow to arouse. She could bear caresses that exhausted him, and he fell asleep in her arms.

Then he found her climbing over him and pouring a little liquid over his penis, something that at first made him smart and then aroused him furiously. He was frightened. His penis seemed to have filled with fire, or with red peppers. He rubbed himself against her flesh, more to ease the burning than out of desire.

He was angry. She was smiling and laughing softly. He began taking her with a rage, driven by a fear that what she had done to him would arouse him for the last time, that it was some sort of enchantment to get the maximum of desire from him, until he died.

She lay back laughing, her white teeth showing, the animal odor of her now affecting him erotically like the smell of musk. She moved with such vigor that he felt she would tear his penis away from him. But now he wanted to subjugate her. He caressed her at the same time.

She was surprised by this. No one seemed to have done this to her before. When he was tired of taking her, after two orgasms, he continued to rub her clitoris, and she enjoyed this, begging for more, opening her legs wide. Then suddenly she turned over, crouched on the bed and swung her ass upward at an incredible angle. She expected him to take her again, but he continued to caress her. After this it was always his hand that she sought. She rubbed against it like a huge cat. During the day, if she met him she would rub her sex against his hand, surreptitiously.

Reynolds said that that night had made white women seem weak to him. He was laughing as he told the story.

His painting had reminded him of the savage woman hiding in the bushes, waiting like a tigress to leap and run away from the men who carried guns. He had painted her in, with her heavy, pointed breasts, her fine, long legs, her slender waist.

I did not know how I could pose for him. But he was thinking of another picture. He said, 'It will be easy. I want you to fall asleep. But you will be wrapped in white sheets. I saw something in Morocco once that I always wanted to paint. A woman had fallen asleep among her silk spools, holding the silk weaving frame with her hennaed feet. You have beautiful eyes, but they'll have to be closed.'

He went into the cabin and brought out sheets which

he draped around me like a robe. He propped me against a wooden box, arranged my body and hands as he wanted them and began to sketch immediately. It was a very hot day. The sheets made me warm, and the pose was so lazy that I actually fell asleep, I don't know for how long. I felt languid and unreal. And then I felt a soft hand between my legs, very soft, caressing me so lightly I had to awaken to make sure I had been touched. Reynolds was bending over me, but with such an expression of delighted gentleness that I did not move. His eyes were tender, his mouth half open.

'Only a caress,' he said, 'just a caress.'

I did not move. I had never felt anything like this hand softly, softly caressing the skin between my legs without touching my sex. He only touched the tips of my pubic hair. Then his hand slipped down to the little valley around the sex. I was growing lax and soft. He leaned over and put his mouth on mine, lightly touching my lips, until my own mouth responded, and only then did he touch the tip of my tongue with his. His hand was moving, exploring, but so softly, it was tantalizing. I was wet, and I knew if he moved just a little more he would feel this. The languor spread all through my body. Each time his tongue touched mine I felt as if there were another little tongue inside of me, flicking out, wanting to be touched too. His hand moved only around my sex, and then around my ass, and it was as if he magnetized the blood to follow the movements of his hands. His finger touched the clitoris so gently, then slipped between the lips of the vulva. He felt the wetness. He touched this with delight, kissing me, lying over me now, and I did not move. The warmth, the smells of plants around me, his mouth over mine affected me like a drug.

'Only a caress,' he repeated gently, his finger moving around my clitoris until the little mound swelled and hardened. Then I felt as if a seed were bursting in me, a joy that made me palpitate under his fingers. I kissed him with gratitude. He was smiling. He said, 'Do you want to caress me?'

I nodded yes, but I did not know what he wanted of me. He unbuttoned his pants and I saw his penis. I took it in my hands. He said, 'Press harder.' He saw then that I did not know how. He took my hand in his and guided me. The little white foam fell all over my hand. He covered himself. He kissed me with the same grateful kiss I had given him after my pleasure.

He said, 'Did you know that a Hindu makes love to his wife ten days before he takes her? For ten days they merely caress and kiss.'

The thought of Ronald's behavior angered him all over again – the way he had wronged me in everybody's eyes. I said, 'Don't get angry. I am happy he did it, because it made me walk away from the village and come here.'

'I loved you as soon as I heard you speak with that accent you have. I felt as if I were traveling again. Your face is so different, your walk, your ways. You remind me of the girl I intended to paint in Fez. I saw her only once, asleep like this. I always dreamed of awakening her as I awakened you.'

'And I always dreamed of being awakened with a caress like this,' I said.

'If you had been awake I might not have dared.'

'You, the adventurer, who lived with a savage woman?'

'I did not really live with the savage woman. That happened to a friend of mine. He was always talking about it, so I always tell it as if it had happened to me. I'm really

46

timid with women. I can knock men down and fight and get drunk, but women intimidate me, even whores. They laugh at me. But this happened exactly as I had always planned it would happen.'

'But the tenth day I will be in New York,' I said laughing.

'The tenth day I will drive you back, if you have to go back. But meanwhile you are my prisoner.'

For ten days we worked out in the open, lying in the sun. The sun would warm my body, as Reynolds waited for me to close my eyes. Sometimes I pretended I wanted him to do more to me. I thought that if I closed my eyes he would take me. I liked the way he would walk up to me, like a hunter, making no sound and lying at my side. Sometimes he lifted my dress first and looked at me for a long time. Then he would touch me lightly, as if he did not want to awaken me, until the moisture came. His fingers would quicken. We kept our mouths together, our tongues caressing. I learned to take his penis in my mouth. This excited him terribly. He would lose all his gentleness, push his penis into my mouth, and I was afraid of choking. Once I bit him, hurt him, but he did not mind. I swallowed the white foam. When he kissed me, our faces were covered with it. The marvelous smell of sex impregnated my fingers. I did not want to wash my hands.

I felt that we shared a magnetic current, but at the same time nothing else bound us together. Reynolds had promised to drive me back to New York. He could not stay in the country much longer. I had to find work.

During the drive back Reynolds stopped the car and we lay on a blanket in the woods, resting. We caressed. He said, 'Are you happy?'

'Yes.'

'Can you continue to be happy, this way? As we are?'

'Why, Reynolds, what is it?'

'Listen, I love you. You know that, but I can't take you. I did that to a girl once, and she got pregnant and had an abortion. She bled to death. Since than I haven't been able to take a woman. I'm afraid. If that should happen to you, I would kill myself.'

I had never thought of things like this. I was silent. We kissed for a long time. For the first time he kissed me between the legs instead of caressing me, kissed me until I felt the orgasm. We were happy. He said, 'This little wound women have . . . it frightens me.'

In New York it was hot and all the artists were still away. I found myself without work. I took up modeling in dress shops. I could easily get work, but when they asked me to go out in the evenings with the buyers I would refuse and lose the job. Finally I was taken into a big place near Thirty-fourth Street where they employed six models. This place was frightening and gray. There were long rows of clothes and a few benches for us to sit on. We waited in our slips, to be ready for quick changes. When our numbers were called, we helped one another dress.

The three men who sold the dress designs often tried to fondle us, squeeze us. We took turns staying during the lunch hour. My greatest fear was that I would be left alone with the man who was most persistent.

Once when Stephen telephoned to ask if he could see me that evening, the man came up behind me and put his hand into my slip to feel my breasts. Not knowing what else to do, I kicked him while I held the phone and tried to go on talking to Stephen. He was not discouraged. Next, he tried to feel my ass. I kicked again.

Stephen was saying, 'What is it, what are you saying?'

I ended the conversation and turned on the man. He was gone.

The buyers admired our physical qualities as much as the dresses. The head salesman was very proud of me and would often say, with his hand on my hair, 'She's an artist's model.'

This made me long to return to posing. I did not want Reynolds or Stephen to find me here in an ugly office building, wearing dresses for ugly salesmen and buyers.

Finally I was called to model at the studio of a South American painter. He had the face of a woman, pale with big black eyes, long black hair, and his gestures were languid and effete. His studio was beautiful – luxuriant rugs, large paintings of nude women, silk hangings; and there was incense burning. He said he had a very intricate pose to do. He was painting a big horse running away with a naked woman. He asked if I had ever ridden on horseback. I said that I had, when I was younger.

'That is marvelous,' he said, 'exactly what I want. Now, I have made a contraption here which gives me the effect I need.'

It was a dummy of a horse without a head, just the body and legs, with a saddle.

He said, 'Take your clothes off first, then I will show you. I have difficulty with this part of the pose. The woman is throwing her body back because the horse is running wild, like this.' He sat on the dummy horse to show me.

By now I no longer felt timid about posing nude. I took my clothes off and sat on the horse, throwing my body backwards, my arms flying, my legs clasping the horse's flanks so as not to fall. The painter approved. He moved away and looked at me. 'It's a hard pose and I do not expect you to keep it long. Just let me know when you get tired.'

He studied me from every side. Then came up close to me and said, 'When I made the drawing, this part of the body showed clearly, here, between the legs.' He touched me lightly as if it were merely part of his work. I curved in my belly a little to throw the hips forward and then he said, 'Now it is fine. Hold it.'

He began to sketch. As I sat there I realized that there was one uncommon detail about the saddle. Most saddles, of course, are shaped to follow the contour of the ass and then rise at the pommel, where they are apt to rub against a woman's sex. I had often experienced both the advantages and the disadvantages of being supported there. Once my garter came loose from the stocking and began to dance around inside my riding trousers. My companions were galloping and I did not want to fall behind, so I continued. The garter, leaping in all directions, finally fell between my sex and the saddle and hurt me. I held on, gritting my teeth. The pain was strangely mixed with a sensation I could not define. I was a girl then and did not know anything about sex. I thought that a woman's sex was inside of her, and I did not know about the clitoris.

When the ride was over, I was in pain. I mentioned what had happened to a girl I knew well, and we both went into the bathroom. She helped me out of my trousers, out of my little belt with the garters on it, and then said, 'Are you hurt? That's a very sensitive spot. Maybe you'll never have any pleasure there if you got hurt.'

I let her look at it. It was red and a little swollen, but not so very painful. What bothered me was her saying I might be deprived of a pleasure by this, a pleasure I did not know. She insisted on bathing it with a wet cotton, fondled me and finally kissed me, 'to make it well'.

I became acutely aware of this part of my body.

Particularly when we rode a long while in the heat, I felt such a warmth and stirring between my legs that all I desired was to get off the horse and let my friend nurse me again. She was always asking me, 'Does it hurt?'

So once I answered, 'Just a little.' We dismounted and went into the bathroom, and she bathed the chaffed spot with cotton and cool water.

And again she fondled me, saying, 'But it does not look sore anymore. Maybe you will be able to enjoy yourself again.'

'I don't know,' I said. 'Do you think it has gone . . . dead . . . from the pain?'

My friend very tenderly leaned over and touched me. 'Does it hurt?'

I lay back and said, 'No, I do not feel anything.'

'Don't you feel this?' she asked with concern, pressing the lips between her fingers.

'No,' I said, watching her.

'Don't you feel this?' She passed her fingers now around the tip of the clitoris, making tiny circles.

'I don't feel anything.'

She became eager to see if I had lost my sensibility and increased her caresses, rubbing the clitoris with one hand while she vibrated the tip with the other. She stroked my pubic hair and tender skin around it. Finally I felt her, wildly, and I began to move. She was panting over me, watching me and saying, 'Wonderful, wonderful, you can feel there . . .'

I was remembering this as I sat on the dummy horse and noticed that the pommel was quite accentuated. So the painter could see what he wanted to paint, I slid forward, and as I did so my sex rubbed against the leather prominence. The painter was observing me.

'Do you like my horse?' he said. 'Do you know that I can make it move?'

'Can you?'

He came near me and set the dummy in motion, and indeed it was perfectly constructed to move like a horse.

'I like it,' I said. 'It reminds me of the times I rode horse-back when I was a girl.' I noticed that he stopped painting now to watch me. The motion of the horse pushed my sex against the saddle even harder and gave me great pleasure. I thought that he would notice it, and so I said, 'Stop it now.' But he smiled and did not stop it. 'Don't you like it?' he said.

I did like it. Each movement brought the leather against my clitoris, and I thought I could not hold back an orgasm if it went on. I begged him to stop. My face was flushed.

The painter was carefully watching me, watching every expression of a pleasure I could not control, and now it increased so that I abandoned myself to the motion of the horse, let myself rub against the leather, until I felt the orgasm and I came, riding this way in front of him.

Only then did I know that he expected it, that he had done all this to see me enjoy it. He knew when to stop the machinery. 'You can rest now,' he said.

Soon after, I went to pose for a woman illustrator, Lena, I had met at a party. She liked company. Actors and actresses came to see her, writers. She painted for magazine covers. The door was always open. People brought drinks. The talk was acid, cruel. It seemed to me that all her friends were caricaturists. Everyone's weaknesses were immediately exposed. Or they exposed their own. One beautiful young man, dressed with great elegance, made no secret of his profession. He sat around at the big hotels, waited for old women who were alone and took them out to dance. Very often they invited him back to their rooms.

Lena made a wry face, 'How can you do it?' she asked him, 'Such old women, how can you possibly get an erection? If I saw a woman like that lying on my bed, I would run away.'

The young man smiled. 'There are so many ways of doing it. One is to close my eyes and to imagine it is not an old woman but a woman I like, and then when my eyes are closed I begin to think how pleasant it will be to be able to pay my rent the next day or to buy a new suit or silk shirts. And as I do this, I keep stroking the woman's sex without looking, and, you know, if your eyes are closed, they feel about the same, more or less. Sometimes, though, when I have difficulty I take drugs. Of course, I know that at this rate my career will last about five years and that at the end of that time I will not be of any use even to a young woman. But by then I will be glad never to see a woman again.

'I certainly envy my Argentine friend, my roommate. He is a handsome, aristocratic man, absolutely effete. Women would love him. When I leave the apartment, do you know what he does? He gets up out of bed, pulls out a small electric iron and an ironing board, takes his pants and begins to press them. As he presses them he imagines how he will come out of the building so impeccably dressed, how he will walk down Fifth Avenue, how somewhere he will spy a beautiful woman, follow the scent of her perfume for many blocks, follow her into crowded elevators, almost touching her. The woman will be wearing a veil and a fur around her neck. Her dress will outline her figure.

'After following her thus through the shops, he will finally speak to her. She will see his handsome face smiling at her and the chivalrous way he has of carrying himself. They will go off together and sit having tea somewhere, then go to the hotel where she is staying. She will invite him to come up with her. They will get into the room and then pull down the shades and lie in the darkness making love.

'As he presses his pants carefully, meticulously, my friend imagines how he will make love to this woman – and it excites him. He knows how he will grip her. He likes to push his penis in from behind and raise the woman's legs, and then get her to turn just a little so that he can see it moving in and out. He likes the woman to squeeze the base of his penis at the same time; her fingers press harder than the mouth of her sex, and that excites him. She will also touch his balls as he moves, and he will touch her clitoris, because that gives her a double pleasure. He will make her gasp and shake from head to foot and beg for more.

'By the time he has envisioned all this standing there, half naked, pressing his pants, my friend has a hard on. It is all he wants. He puts away the pants, the iron and the ironing board, and he gets into bed again, lying back and smoking, thinking over this scene until each detail of it is perfect and a drop of semen appears at the head of his penis, which he strokes while he lies smoking and dreaming of pursuing other women.

'I envy him because he can get so much excitement from thinking all this. He questions me. He wants to know how my women are made, how they behave . . .'

Lena laughed. She said, 'It's hot. I will take my corset off.' And she went into the alcove. When she came back her body looked free and lax. She sat down, crossed her bare legs, her blouse half-open. One of her friends sat where he could see her.

Another one, a handsome man, stood near me as I was posing and whispered compliments. He said, 'I love you because you remind me of Europe – Paris especially. I don't know what there is about Paris, but there is sensuality in the air there. It is contagious. It is such a human city. I don't know whether it is because couples are always kissing in the streets, at tables in the cafés, in the movies, in the parks. They embrace each other so freely. They stop for long complete kisses in the middle of the sidewalk, at the subway entrances. Perhaps it is that, or the softness of the air. I don't know. In the dark, in each doorway at night there is a man and a woman almost melted into one another. The whores watch for you every moment . . . they touch you.

'One day I was standing on a platform bus, looking up idly at the houses. I saw a window open and a man and woman lying on a bed. The woman was sitting over the man.

'At five o'clock in the afternoon it becomes unbearable. There is love and desire in the air. Everybody is in the streets. The cafés are full. In the movies there are little boxes that are completely dark and curtained off so that you can make love on the floor while the movie is going on and not be seen. It is all so open, so easy. No police to interfere. A woman friend of mine who was followed and annoyed by a man complained to the policeman at the corner. He laughed and said, "You'll be sorrier the day no man wants to annoy you, won't you? After all, you should be thankful instead of getting angry." And he would not help her.'

Then my admirer said in a lower voice, 'Will you come and have dinner with me and go to the theatre?'

He became my first real lover. I forgot Reynolds and Stephen. They now seem like children to me.

POCKET PENGUINS

POCKET PENGUINS